A Lasting Heritage for Your Children

A Father's Legacy

Your Life Story in
Your Own Words

WORD PUBLISHING
Dallas • London • Vancouver • Melbourne

A J. Countryman Book

*Designed by Koechel Peterson Design, Inc.,
Minneapolis, Minnesota*

Edited by Terri Gibbs

ISBN: 0-8499-5275-1

Printed and bound in the United States of America

89 RRD 987

Contents

Introduction

. . . .

"What grade did you get in high school English, Dad?"
"What did you do on your first date?" Sound familiar?
Your son or daughter has probably asked these questions
and many more. Why? Curiosity partly, but mostly
because they care—about you. They want to know what
you did when you were growing up because they want to
know you.

That is the purpose of this book, which is a book about
you—your family history, your childhood memories,
humorous incidents, and meaningful traditions from your
life. It is a personal biography just waiting to be written.
Yes, there are planes to catch, meetings to attend, grass to
mow, and the car to wash, but those are not a legacy you
can pass on to your child. This book is.

Presented in a twelve-month format, this journal provides
an array of questions your son or daughter might ask
with space for your answers. Questions like, "Describe
the most fun you ever had on a Fourth of July."

Or "When you went to a ball game as a boy, what kind of food did you eat?" Or "What is the nicest thing you ever did for your mother and father?"

These questions will help you write down the special memories, thoughts, and ideas you want to share with your children. You may choose to complete the journal in a few days, a few weeks, or throughout the course of the year. When you have filled in all of the pages you will have a loving memoir—a spiritual legacy—to pass on to your children. They will cherish this book about you for a lifetime.

This book is for fathers of all ages, because it is never too early or too late to share your life with those you love. May *A Father's Legacy* draw you closer to your children as you share this memoir of your life...straight from your heart to theirs.

Personal Portrait

your full given name _____.

your date of birth _____.

your place of birth _____.

your mother's full name _____.

  the place and date of her birth _____.

your father's full name _____.

  the place and date of his birth _____.

the names of your paternal grandparents _____.

  the places and dates of their births _____.

the names of your maternal grandparents _____.

  the places and dates of their births _____.

the names of your siblings _____.

  the places and dates of their births _____.

_____.

_____.

the date and place of your marriage _____.

the full given name of your wife _____.

the names and birth dates of your children _____.

_____.

_____.

What is your favorite?

sport _____ . Bible verse _____ .

book _____ . hymn or song _____ .

leisure activity _____ . vacation spot _____ .

dessert _____ . type of food _____ .

author _____ . sports team _____ .

January

Our stories are

inextricably interwoven.

What you do is part of my story;

what I do is part of yours.

— DANIEL TAYLOR

What did you enjoy doing most as a child?
Did you prefer doing it alone or with someone else?

_____

_____

_____

_____

_____

_____

_____

_____

_____

_____

_____

_____

_____

_____

_____

_____

_____

_____

_____

_____

_____

_____

_____

_____

—*January*—

W

ho gave you your name and why?
Did you have a nickname? How did you get it? _____

_____

_____

_____

_____

_____

_____

_____

_____

_____

_____

_____

_____

_____

_____

_____

_____

_____

_____

_____

_____

_____

_____

_____

_____

*D*escribe your childhood home.
What was your favorite room?

_____

_____

_____

_____

_____

_____

_____

_____

_____

_____

_____

_____

_____

_____

_____

_____

_____

_____

_____

_____

_____

_____

_____

_____

_____

_____

_____

Were you baptized or dedicated as an infant? If so, where and by whom? _____

_____

_____

_____

_____

_____

_____

_____

_____

_____

_____

_____

_____

_____

_____

_____

_____

_____

_____

_____

_____

_____

_____

_____

_____

_____

_____

Did you attend church as a young boy?
What are your earliest memories of church? _____

_____

_____

_____

_____

_____

_____

_____

_____

_____

_____

_____

_____

_____

_____

_____

_____

_____

_____

_____

_____

_____

_____

_____

_____

_____

_____

Where did your father go to work every day and what did he do? Did his work interest you?

Did your mother have a job
or did she work at home?

—January—

*W*hat was your favorite sport or outdoor activity? Why was this your favorite?

_____

_____

_____

_____

_____

_____

_____

_____

_____

_____

_____

_____

_____

_____

_____

_____

_____

_____

_____

_____

_____

_____

—*January*—

Did you pray as a young boy?
If so, can you remember a specific prayer?
Who taught you to pray? _____.

. _____
. _____
. _____
. _____
. _____
. _____
. _____
. _____
. _____
. _____
. _____
. _____
. _____
. _____
. _____
. _____
. _____
. _____
. _____
. _____
. _____
. _____
. _____

Where was your childhood home located?
Did you enjoy living there?

Describe your grandparents.
What did you enjoy most about them?

_____

_____

_____

_____

_____

_____

_____

_____

_____

_____

_____

_____

_____

_____

_____

_____

_____

_____

_____

_____

_____

_____

_____

_____

_____

Can you remember being afraid as a boy?
What was your greatest fear?
How did you deal with it?

Recall for me five
of the most important lessons
you have learned in life.

_____
_____
_____
_____
_____
_____
_____
_____
_____
_____
_____
_____
_____
_____
_____
_____
_____

February

Gratitude is the
memory of the heart.

———

MASSIEU

—February—

Did the pastor or a visiting missionary ever eat dinner at your house? Did they have an impact on your life? _____ .

_____
_____
_____
_____
_____
_____
_____
_____
_____
_____
_____
_____
_____
_____
_____
_____
_____
_____
_____
_____
_____
_____

*Did you ever feel that
God had a special calling on your life?* _____

_____

_____

_____

_____

_____

_____

_____

_____

_____

_____

_____

_____

_____

_____

_____

_____

_____

_____

_____

_____

_____

—February—

Describe the most memorable
Valentine you ever received.
Who sent it to you? _____

_____

_____

_____

_____

_____

_____

_____

_____

_____

_____

_____

_____

_____

_____

_____

_____

_____

_____

_____

_____

_____

_____

_____

—*February*—

How far did you have to travel to attend elementary, junior high, and high school, and how did you get there? _____ .

_____

_____

_____

_____

_____

_____

_____

_____

_____

_____

_____

_____

_____

_____

_____

_____

_____

_____

_____

_____

_____

_____

Who gave you your first Bible
and how old where you when you received it.
How did it influence your life? _____

_____

_____

_____

_____

_____

_____

_____

_____

_____

_____

_____

_____

_____

_____

_____

_____

_____

_____

_____

_____

_____

When did you become a Christian?
How did your life change? _____

_____

_____

_____

_____

_____

_____

_____

_____

_____

_____

_____

_____

_____

_____

_____

_____

_____

_____

_____

_____

_____

_____

_____

Did you go to ball games as a boy?
What kind of food did you eat?

*W*hen you were growing up, did you
have any animals? What were their names?
Was it important to you to have a pet? _____.

_____
_____
_____
_____
_____
_____
_____
_____
_____
_____
_____
_____
_____
_____
_____
_____
_____
_____
_____
_____
_____
_____
_____

Tell me about your mother's cooking.
Can you recall your favorite meal?
What made it your favorite? _____.

_____
_____
_____
_____
_____
_____
_____
_____
_____
_____
_____
_____
_____
_____
_____
_____
_____
_____
_____
_____

—February—

*id you ever get into fights with others kids?
Did you ever start a fight? Or stop one?* _____

_____

_____

_____

_____

_____

_____

_____

_____

_____

_____

_____

_____

_____

_____

_____

_____

_____

_____

_____

_____

_____

_____

_____

_____

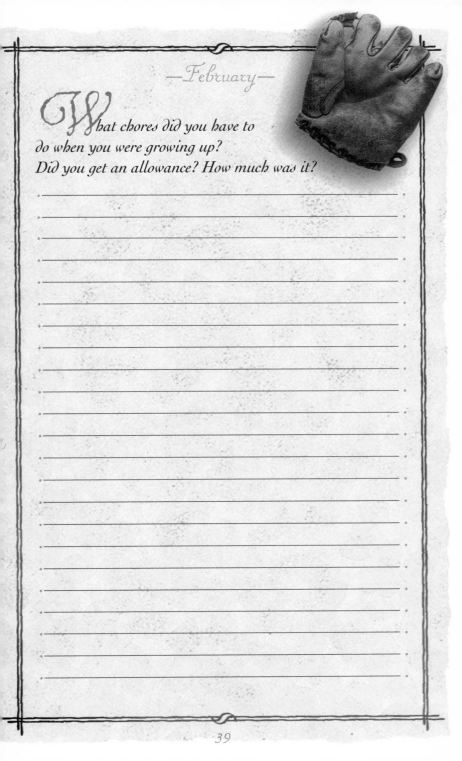

—February—

What chores did you have to do when you were growing up? Did you get an allowance? How much was it?

Who gave you your first job?
What kind of job was it?
*How much money did you make?*_____.

_____
_____
_____
_____
_____
_____
_____
_____
_____
_____
_____
_____
_____
_____
_____
_____
_____
_____
_____
_____
_____
_____

Share your idea of
what makes a good friend.

March

We have one life to live —
and one chance to live it in the
richest way possible.

JUDITH THURMAN

*D*o you remember your first communion?
What influence did it have on you and your family?

_____

_____

_____

_____

_____

_____

_____

_____

_____

_____

_____

_____

_____

_____

_____

_____

_____

_____

_____

_____

_____

_____

_____

_____

_____

_____

Describe your favorite
pastime or hobby as a child.

What mischievous prank did
you pull on someone? How did it affect you?

_____
_____
_____
_____
_____
_____
_____
_____
_____
_____
_____
_____
_____
_____
_____
_____
_____
_____
_____
_____
_____
_____
_____
_____
_____
_____

Did you have a television when you were growing up? What was your favorite program? Why?

What were some crazy fads from your school days? Did you participate in them? Why or why not?

_____
_____
_____
_____
_____
_____
_____
_____
_____
_____
_____
_____
_____
_____
_____
_____
_____
_____
_____
_____
_____
_____
_____
_____
_____
_____

Who was your favorite teacher?
How did that teacher influence your life? _____

_____

_____

_____

_____

_____

_____

_____

_____

_____

_____

_____

_____

_____

_____

_____

_____

_____

_____

_____

_____

_____

_____

_____

_____

—March—

Did you ever have a special hideaway or clubhouse? Describe it for me.

In high school, what extracurricular activities did you enjoy most? Why did you choose those activities? _____

_____
_____
_____
_____
_____
_____
_____
_____
_____
_____
_____
_____
_____
_____
_____
_____
_____
_____
_____
_____
_____
_____
_____
_____
_____

What is the nicest thing you ever did for your mother and father?

*Did you admire a famous person?
What made that person admirable?*

—*March*—

*When did you have your first date?
Tell me about it.*

—*March*—

*W*hat do you remember
about your first kiss? _____

_____
_____
_____
_____
_____
_____
_____
_____
_____
_____
_____
_____
_____
_____
_____
_____
_____
_____
_____
_____
_____
_____
_____
_____

Share some of
your insights for working
well with others.

_____

_____

_____

_____

_____

_____

_____

_____

_____

_____

_____

_____

_____

_____

_____

_____

_____

April

It is in the shelter

of each other that the people live.

IRISH PROVERB

—*April*—

*D*id you enjoy reading as a boy?
What were some of the most memorable books you read?

—*April*—

*W*hat were your family finances like when
you were growing up? How did that affect you? _____

_____
_____
_____
_____
_____
_____
_____
_____
_____
_____
_____
_____
_____
_____
_____
_____
_____
_____
_____
_____
_____
_____
_____
_____
_____

—April—

Was there a special person
who helped you in your Christian walk?
Share something about that person. _____

_____
_____
_____
_____
_____
_____
_____
_____
_____
_____
_____
_____
_____
_____
_____
_____
_____
_____
_____
_____
_____
_____
_____
_____

When did you first learn about sex?
Would you recommend the same for young people today?
Why or why not? _____

_____

_____

_____

_____

_____

_____

_____

_____

_____

_____

_____

_____

_____

_____

_____

_____

_____

_____

_____

_____

_____

_____

_____

_____

_____

—April—

*As a teenager did you rebel or do things
your parents wouldn't have approved of?
How do you feel about that now?* _____

_____
_____
_____
_____
_____
_____
_____
_____
_____
_____
_____
_____
_____
_____
_____
_____
_____
_____
_____
_____
_____
_____
_____
_____

—April—

*L*ist three things you wish you had done during
your junior high and high school years, but didn't.

What did your family like to do on weekends? Describe one particularly memorable one.

_____
_____
_____
_____
_____
_____
_____
_____
_____
_____
_____
_____
_____
_____
_____
_____
_____
_____
_____
_____
_____
_____
_____
_____
_____
_____
_____
_____
_____

—*April*—

During childhood, who was your best friend?
Share some of your fondest memories of fun times together.

_____
_____
_____
_____
_____
_____
_____
_____
_____
_____
_____
_____
_____
_____
_____
_____
_____
_____
_____
_____
_____
_____
_____
_____

—*April*—

Did you ever keep a scrapbook of photos, autographs, or memories of special occasions? Describe what this meant to you. _____ .

_____ .
_____ .
_____ .
_____ .
_____ .
_____ .
_____ .
_____ .
_____ .
_____ .
_____ .
_____ .
_____ .
_____ .
_____ .
_____ .
_____ .
_____ .
_____ .
_____ .
_____ .
_____ .
_____ .

What is your favorite memory of your mother? Why is it so special to you?

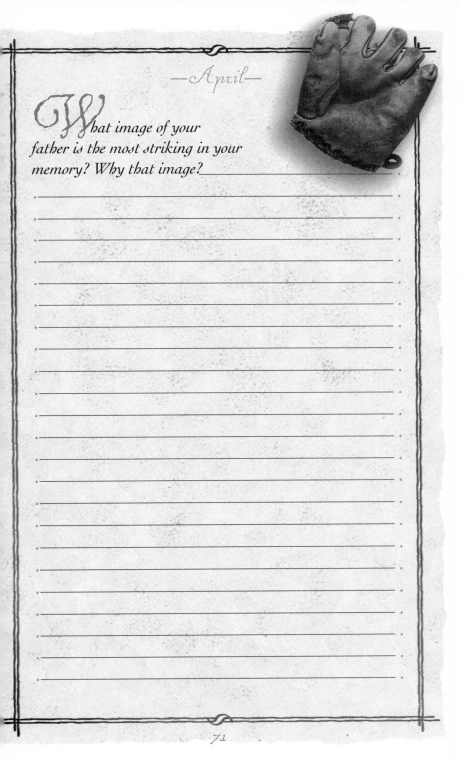

—April—

$\mathcal{W}$hat image of your
father is the most striking in your
memory? Why that image?

List one special memory about each of your brothers and sisters.

Share with me your
father's attitude toward life
and how that affected you.

_____
_____
_____
_____
_____
_____
_____
_____
_____
_____
_____
_____
_____
_____
_____
_____
_____
_____

May

*W*ho, being loved, is poor?

— ❦ —

OSCAR WILDE

—May—

If you were to find an old toy box in your attic, what toys would you remember most fondly? Why?

—*May*—

How old were you when you understood that God loves you? How did that affect your life?

*D*escribe a time in your life when you feel God led you in an unusual way.

What kind of car did your family drive?
Were you proud of it or embarrassed by it? Why?

— *May* —

*D*id you ever go to a dance?
Tell me about it.

—*May*—

*H*ow often did your family go to church?
What pastor or Sunday school teacher do you
remember most? How did that person influence you?

_____
_____
_____
_____
_____
_____
_____
_____
_____
_____
_____
_____
_____
_____
_____
_____
_____
_____
_____
_____
_____
_____

*D*id your family attend family reunions?
What activities did everyone enjoy? Tell me about
your favorite cousins, aunts, or uncles. _____ .

_____ .
_____ .
_____ .
_____ .
_____ .
_____ .
_____ .
_____ .
_____ .
_____ .
_____ .
_____ .
_____ .
_____ .
_____ .
_____ .
_____ .
_____ .
_____ .
_____ .
_____ .
_____ .
_____ .
_____ .
_____ .
_____ .
_____ .
_____ .

—May—

When you were young, did you
ever go to a funeral? How did that affect you.

_____
_____
_____
_____
_____
_____
_____
_____
_____
_____
_____
_____
_____
_____
_____
_____
_____
_____
_____
_____
_____
_____
_____
_____
_____

*If you had brothers and sisters,
did you feel your parents treated you all the same?
Why or why not? If you were an only child,
did you wish for brothers and sisters? Why?* _____

_____

_____

_____

_____

_____

_____

_____

_____

_____

_____

_____

_____

_____

_____

_____

_____

_____

_____

_____

_____

_____

Did your high school have college or career days?
What field interested you most?
What did you want to become when you grew up? _____

_____

_____

_____

_____

_____

_____

_____

_____

_____

_____

_____

_____

_____

_____

_____

_____

_____

_____

_____

_____

_____

_____

_____

_____

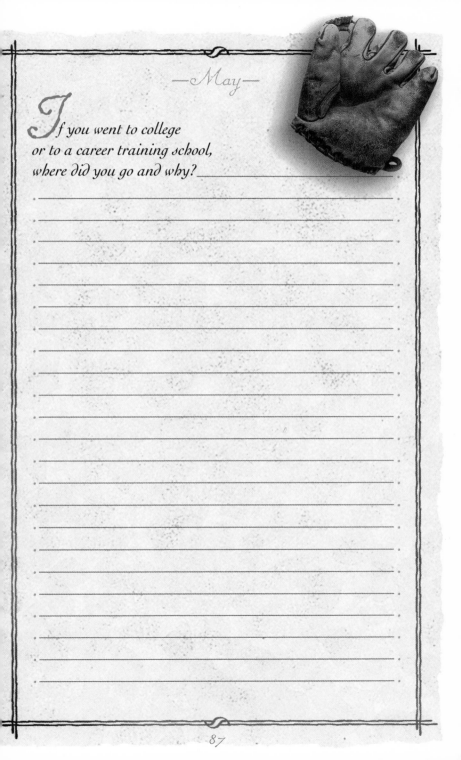

—May—

If you went to college or to a career training school, where did you go and why?

Where did you live when you were going to college or developing a career? Describe an unforgettable experience from that time in your life. _____

_____

_____

_____

_____

_____

_____

_____

_____

_____

_____

_____

_____

_____

_____

_____

_____

_____

_____

_____

_____

_____

_____

_____

_____

_____

_____

Share some principles from Scripture on which you have chosen to build your life.

_____
_____
_____
_____
_____
_____
_____
_____
_____
_____
_____
_____
_____
_____
_____
_____
_____
_____

June

The linking of generations,

the historical lineage of family,

the sharing of love . . .

give purpose to life.

GEORGE LANDBERG

If you learned to play a musical instrument, tell me your memories of lessons, practice, and your music teacher. If not, what instrument did you want to play and why?

What were your youthful goals and ambitions for life? Which ones have you been able to fulfill?

_____

_____

_____

_____

_____

_____

_____

_____

_____

_____

_____

_____

_____

_____

_____

_____

_____

_____

_____

_____

_____

_____

_____

*H*ow old were you when you
met Mom? What attracted you to her?

_____

_____

_____

_____

_____

_____

_____

_____

_____

_____

_____

_____

_____

_____

_____

_____

_____

_____

_____

_____

_____

_____

_____

_____

_____

_____

When did you know that Mom was the
"one and only one" for you? How did you know?

_____
_____
_____
_____
_____
_____
_____
_____
_____
_____
_____
_____
_____
_____
_____
_____
_____
_____
_____
_____
_____
_____
_____

Share a memory about the way you proposed to Mom. _____

_____
_____
_____
_____
_____
_____
_____
_____
_____
_____
_____
_____
_____
_____
_____
_____
_____
_____
_____
_____
_____
_____
_____
_____
_____
_____

*Tell me about your wedding day.
What happened? How did you feel?
Were you nervous, scared, happy?* _____

_____
_____
_____
_____
_____
_____
_____
_____
_____
_____
_____
_____
_____
_____
_____
_____
_____
_____
_____
_____
_____
_____

*W*here did you go on your honeymoon?
Describe at least one humorous thing that
happened to you and Mom. _____

_____
_____
_____
_____
_____
_____
_____
_____
_____
_____
_____
_____
_____
_____
_____
_____
_____
_____
_____
_____
_____
_____
_____

*D*o you remember the first meals Mom
cooked for you? Do you dare comment on them?

Describe where you and Mom
lived after you got married. What was the
view like from the kitchen window? _____ .

_____
_____
_____
_____
_____
_____
_____
_____
_____
_____
_____
_____
_____
_____
_____
_____
_____
_____
_____
_____
_____
_____

When did you and Mom start talking about having children? Why did you want children—or did you?

_____

_____

_____

_____

_____

_____

_____

_____

_____

_____

_____

_____

_____

_____

_____

_____

_____

_____

_____

_____

_____

_____

_____

_____

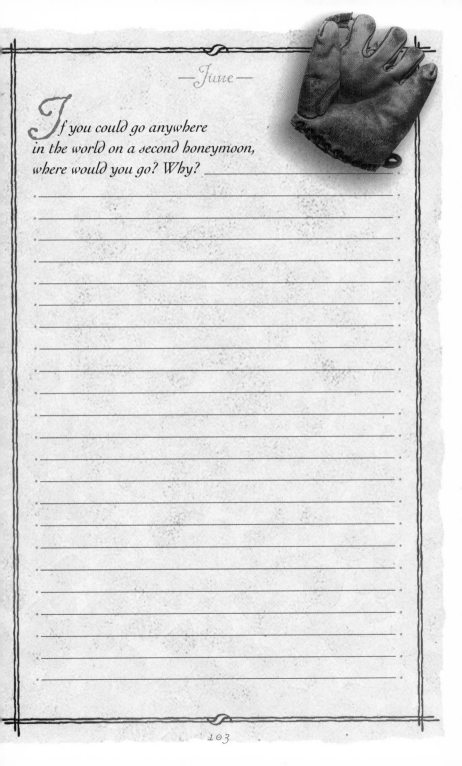

—June—

If you could go anywhere in the world on a second honeymoon, where would you go? Why?

What do you love best about Mom now?

_____

. _____

. _____

. _____

. _____

. _____

. _____

. _____

. _____

. _____

. _____

. _____

. _____

. _____

. _____

. _____

. _____

. _____

. _____

. _____

. _____

. _____

. _____

. _____

Record here your ideas on what it takes for a husband and wife to maintain a healthy marriage.

_____
_____
_____
_____
_____
_____
_____
_____
_____
_____
_____
_____
_____
_____
_____
_____
_____
_____
_____
_____
_____

July

Somehow, year after year,
Dad managed to take us on vacations
he couldn't afford to provide, in order
to make memories that we couldn't
afford to be without.

RICHARD EXLEY

—*July*—

Describe the most fun you ever had on a Fourth of July.

Tell me about your family summer outings when you were young. Did you go camping? Fishing? Swimming?

—July—

Did you ever travel abroad?
How old were you and where did you go?

Who is the most interesting foreigner
you have ever met? What did this person help
you learn about his or her culture? _____

_____
_____
_____
_____
_____
_____
_____
_____
_____
_____
_____
_____
_____
_____
_____
_____
_____
_____
_____
_____
_____
_____
_____

If you served in the armed forces,
describe how your time in the service affected your life.
If you did not serve, how did this affect your life? _____ .

*H*ave you ever believed so strongly in a cause
that you marched in a rally or demonstrated in protest?
What was the cause? Why was it important to you? _____

_____
_____
_____
_____
_____
_____
_____
_____
_____
_____
_____
_____
_____
_____
_____
_____
_____
_____
_____
_____
_____
_____
_____

What is the gutsiest thing you ever did in your life? Why did you do it?

Where do you stand politically? Do you lean toward the left or the right? Who, if anyone, has most greatly influenced your current political views?

id a tragedy ever strike your family?
If so, how did it affect you? _____

_____

_____

_____

_____

_____

_____

_____

_____

_____

_____

_____

_____

_____

_____

_____

_____

_____

_____

_____

_____

_____

_____

_____

_____

What is the best movie you've ever seen?
If you could play one of the characters in the film,
whom would you choose, and why?_____.

_____
_____
_____
_____
_____
_____
_____
_____
_____
_____
_____
_____
_____
_____
_____
_____
_____
_____
_____
_____
_____
_____
_____
_____
_____

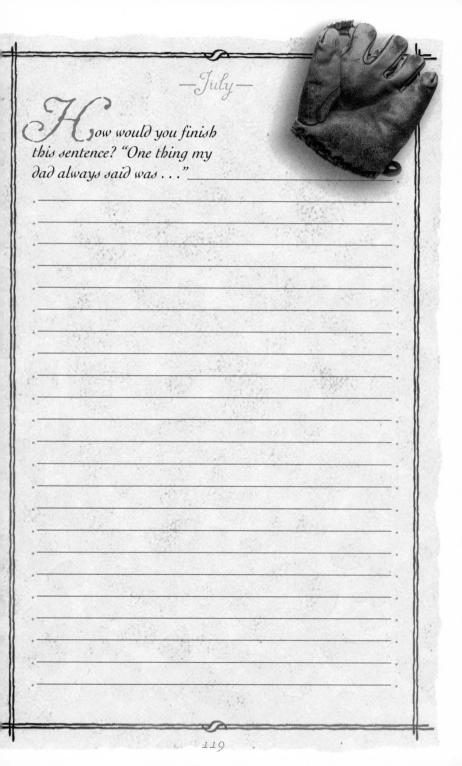

*H*ow would you finish this sentence? "One thing my dad always said was . . ."

Did you ever go to summer camp?
Camping with the Boy Scouts?
Share one unforgettable memory. _____

_____

_____

_____

_____

_____

_____

_____

_____

_____

_____

_____

_____

_____

_____

_____

_____

_____

_____

_____

_____

_____

_____

_____

_____

Share a favorite poem,
passage of writing, or some
quotes that have been especially
meaningful in your life.

_____
_____
_____
_____
_____
_____
_____
_____
_____
_____
_____
_____
_____
_____
_____
_____

August

When I come home
from work and see those little noses
pressed against the window pane,
then I know I am a success.

PAUL FAULKNER

*I*s there any one book or author who helped you to
develop a philosophy of life? Share some of those insights.

_____

_____

_____

_____

_____

_____

_____

_____

_____

_____

_____

_____

_____

_____

_____

_____

_____

_____

_____

_____

_____

*H*ow have your ideas about
God changed from when you were young?

_____

_____

_____

_____

_____

_____

_____

_____

_____

_____

_____

_____

_____

_____

_____

_____

_____

_____

_____

_____

_____

_____

_____

_____

What kind of outdoor work do you enjoy? Dislike?

_____

_____

_____

_____

_____

_____

_____

_____

_____

_____

_____

_____

_____

_____

_____

_____

_____

_____

_____

_____

_____

_____

_____

_____

_____

What is your favorite way to spend a day of leisure?

—August—

When did you learn how to ride a bike, or to water ski, snow ski, roller skate, or sail? Share your memories of the experience. _____

_____
_____
_____
_____
_____
_____
_____
_____
_____
_____
_____
_____
_____
_____
_____
_____
_____
_____
_____
_____
_____
_____
_____
_____

*D*id you ever milk a cow or spend time
on a farm or in the country? Tell me about it.

What places in the world would you still like to visit? Why?

_____

_____

_____

_____

_____

_____

_____

_____

_____

_____

_____

_____

_____

_____

_____

_____

_____

_____

_____

_____

_____

_____

_____

_____

_____

_____

_____

_____

_____

_____

_____

_____

*I*s there any childhood fear that still haunts
you? How do you deal with this fear? _____

_____
_____
_____
_____
_____
_____
_____
_____
_____
_____
_____
_____
_____
_____
_____
_____
_____
_____
_____
_____
_____
_____
_____

How do you enjoy helping people?
Share about a time when you helped someone in need.

If you could carve one more face on Mt. Rushmore, whose face would it be? Why?

—August—

In what ways are you like
your mother? Like your father?

*L*ooking back in life, what one thing would you have done differently? Why? _____

_____
_____
_____
_____
_____
_____
_____
_____
_____
_____
_____
_____
_____
_____
_____
_____
_____
_____
_____
_____
_____
_____
_____
_____
_____
_____

Share some tips for a great vacation.

September

What lies behind
us and what lies before us
are tiny matters compared
to what lies within us.

RALPH WALDO EMERSON

*D*id you learn mechanics or woodworking
as a young person? How and when? What were
some of your most memorable projects?_____.

_____

_____

_____

_____

_____

_____

_____

_____

_____

_____

_____

_____

_____

_____

_____

_____

_____

_____

_____

_____

_____

Tell about a special outing you took with your dad. What makes this a poignant memory for you?

As a young person did you volunteer for work in church, community, or social services? Tell me about it.

When did you move away from home?
Describe where you lived and how you felt about it.

Tell me about some of your closest friends
after you and Mom got married. What were
some of the fun things you would do together? _____.

_____
_____
_____
_____
_____
_____
_____
_____
_____
_____
_____
_____
_____
_____
_____
_____
_____
_____
_____
_____
_____
_____
_____

What are your spiritual strengths?

_____

·_____·

·_____·

·_____·

·_____·

·_____·

·_____·

·_____·

·_____·

·_____·

·_____·

·_____·

·_____·

·_____·

·_____·

·_____·

·_____·

·_____·

·_____·

·_____·

·_____·

·_____·

·_____·

·_____·

How would you like to grow spiritually?

What special talents did your parents nurture in you? How have you developed those talents?

—September—

What would you still like to learn to do? Why?

_____

._____

._____

._____

._____

._____

._____

._____

._____

._____

._____

._____

._____

._____

._____

._____

._____

._____

._____

._____

._____

._____

._____

What did you enjoy doing with your mom? Share a special time with her. _____

_____

_____

_____

_____

_____

_____

_____

_____

_____

_____

_____

_____

_____

_____

_____

_____

_____

_____

_____

_____

_____

_____

_____

_____

_____

How would you describe yourself: tender-hearted or tough-minded?

If you were to write a book about Mom, how would you title the book? The first few chapters?

How do you describe "success"?

October

Life's journey is circular,
it appears. The years don't
carry us away from our fathers—
they return us to them.

Michel Marriott

Who are some of the best public speakers you
have ever heard? Why did they impress you?

_____

_____

_____

_____

_____

_____

_____

_____

_____

_____

_____

_____

_____

_____

_____

_____

_____

_____

_____

_____

_____

_____

_____

_____

*If you could have two hours of conversation
with anyone on earth, who would that be?
Why that person? What would you talk about?*

*W*hat spiritual legacy
would you like to leave for others?
Why is this important to you? _____

. _____ .

. _____ .

. _____ .

. _____ .

. _____ .

. _____ .

. _____ .

. _____ .

. _____ .

. _____ .

. _____ .

. _____ .

. _____ .

. _____ .

. _____ .

. _____ .

. _____ .

. _____ .

. _____ .

. _____ .

. _____ .

. _____ .

. _____ .

—*October*—

*S*hare a hilarious travel experience.

—October—

*W*hat Bible verse or Scripture puzzles you the most? Which blesses you the most? Why? _____

_____
_____
_____
_____
_____
_____
_____
_____
_____
_____
_____
_____
_____
_____
_____
_____
_____
_____
_____
_____
_____
_____
_____
_____
_____

Have you ever been in an accident, had surgery or a long illness? How did this affect your outlook on life?

—October—

Do you have a favorite sports team?
Why is that one your favorite?

—October—

What responsibilities did your parents require of you as a child? How did this affect your growth and development? How you raised your children? _____

_____
_____
_____
_____
_____
_____
_____
_____
_____
_____
_____
_____
_____
_____
_____
_____
_____
_____
_____
_____
_____

What is the most frightening thing that has ever happened to you? How did you handle the experience?

What events in life have strengthened
or weakened your belief in prayer. _____

_____

_____

_____

_____

_____

_____

_____

_____

_____

_____

_____

_____

_____

_____

_____

_____

_____

_____

_____

_____

_____

_____

_____

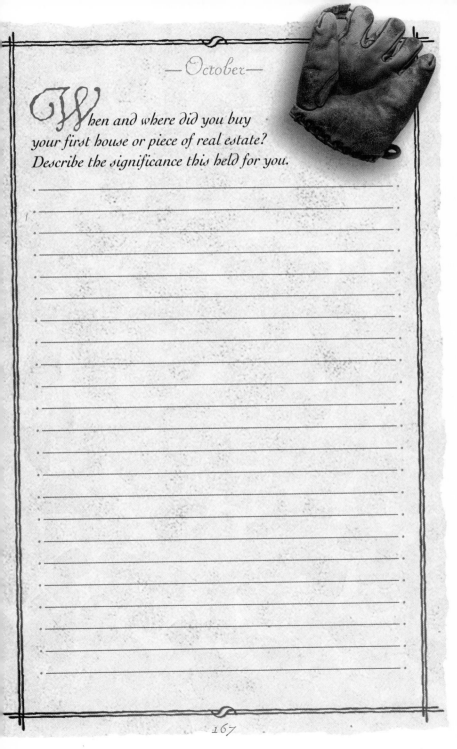

—*October*—

*When and where did you buy
your first house or piece of real estate?
Describe the significance this held for you.*

—*October*—

What is the strangest thing you have ever seen?

_____

Share some of your ideas on how to develop and maintain good physical health.

_____
_____
_____
_____
_____
_____
_____
_____
_____
_____
_____
_____
_____
_____
_____
_____
_____
_____

November

*G*od calls each
generation to pass down
spiritual truth to the next.

—◦—

DENNIS RAINEY

As a teenager, did you belong to a club or church youth group? Tell me about the individuals in the group who were most significant to you.

*What is your most treasured possession and why?*_____

_____

_____

_____

_____

_____

_____

_____

_____

_____

_____

_____

_____

_____

_____

_____

_____

_____

_____

_____

_____

_____

_____

What Bible character
would you most like to meet? Why?

What two people have made the greatest spiritual impact on your life? What made them so significant to you?

When you were a new father,
what was your greatest fear? Your greatest joy?

_____
_____
_____
_____
_____
_____
_____
_____
_____
_____
_____
_____
_____
_____
_____
_____
_____
_____
_____
_____
_____
_____
_____
_____
_____
_____

What is your most vivid memory about my childhood? _____

_____

_____

_____

_____

_____

_____

_____

_____

_____

_____

_____

_____

_____

_____

_____

_____

_____

_____

_____

_____

_____

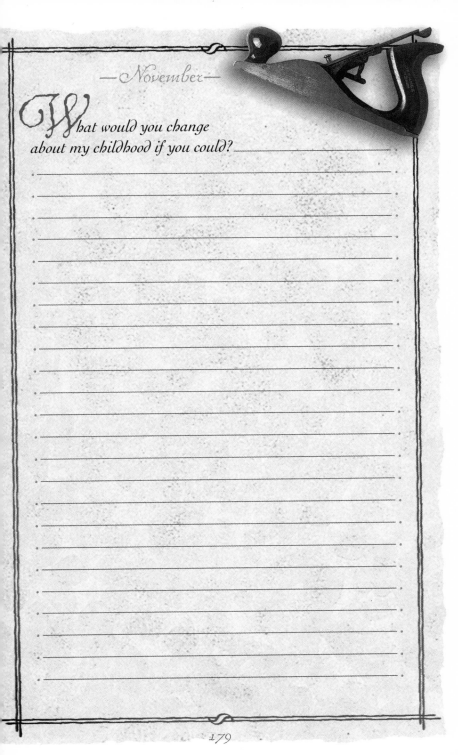

—November—

What would you change
about my childhood if you could?

Describe a fond Thanksgiving memory. What makes this special to you?

_____

_____
_____
_____
_____
_____
_____
_____
_____
_____
_____
_____
_____
_____
_____
_____
_____
_____
_____
_____
_____
_____
_____
_____

What are some things from your
childhood that you are thankful for? _____

_____

_____

_____

_____

_____

_____

_____

_____

_____

_____

_____

_____

_____

_____

_____

_____

_____

_____

_____

_____

_____

_____

_____

_____

What childhood memory first comes to mind when you think about winter? How do you respond to that memory?

_____
_____
_____
_____
_____
_____
_____
_____
_____
_____
_____
_____
_____
_____
_____
_____
_____
_____
_____
_____
_____
_____
_____
_____
_____
_____

*D*escribe the most interesting person you ever met. What were the qualities that made that individual so outstanding?

What family customs or traditions would you like to pass on to your children and grandchildren. Why are they important to you? _____

._____
._____
._____
._____
._____
._____
._____
._____
._____
._____
._____
._____
._____
._____
._____
._____
._____
._____
._____
._____
._____
._____
._____

Tell me what four things
you would never leave behind
on a trip and explain why.

_____

_____

_____

_____

_____

_____

_____

_____

_____

_____

_____

_____

_____

_____

_____

_____

December

Those who loved you
and were helped by you will
remember you. So carve your name
on hearts and not on marble.

—~—

C. H. SPURGEON

Describe some Christmas traditions from your childhood and tell how they have influenced your life.

_____
_____
_____
_____
_____
_____
_____
_____
_____
_____
_____
_____
_____
_____
_____
_____
_____
_____
_____
_____
_____
_____
_____

—December—

Were you ever in a Christmas program? How did you respond to the experience?

190

—December—

What is the best Christmas present you ever received? Why was that the best?

—December—

*T*ell about a memorable
Christmas visit with relatives.

—December—

What is your favorite Christmas carol? Why?

_____
_____
_____
_____
_____
_____
_____
_____
_____
_____
_____
_____
_____
_____
_____
_____
_____
_____
_____
_____
_____
_____
_____
_____
_____
_____
_____
_____

What would be the most wonderful gift you could receive? Why?

_____
_____
_____
_____
_____
_____
_____
_____
_____
_____
_____
_____
_____
_____
_____
_____
_____
_____
_____
_____
_____
_____
_____
_____
_____

Tell me about a time when
God answered a specific prayer for you.

What would you like to see happen in the next ten years in your life? In the world?

As you look back in life, name three of the most fantastic changes that have taken place in the world. How have these affected your life? _____ .

_____
_____
_____
_____
_____
_____
_____
_____
_____
_____
_____
_____
_____
_____
_____
_____
_____
_____
_____
_____
_____
_____

Where would you still like to go and what would you like to do once you got there?

_____

_____
_____
_____
_____
_____
_____
_____
_____
_____
_____
_____
_____
_____
_____
_____
_____
_____
_____
_____
_____
_____
_____
_____
_____
_____

What is your favorite way
to spend a rainy day?

What word best describes your life?
Explain why.

_____

_____

_____

_____

_____

_____

_____

_____

_____

_____

_____

_____

_____

_____

_____

_____

_____

_____

_____

_____

_____

_____

_____

_____

_____

_____

_____

_____

What advice about life do you want others to remember?

Notes

Notes

Notes

Photos

Photos

Photos

Photos